STRIKE ACES

STRIKE ACES

Lindsay Peacock

GUILD PUBLISHING
LONDON · NEW YORK · SYDNEY · TORONTO

A Salamander Book

This edition published 1989
by Guild Publishing
by arrangement with
Salamander Books

CN 3554

Photo credits
Jacket: Frank Mormillo/IDI **Endpapers:** Joe Cupido/IDI **Page 1:** Lindsay Peacock **2/3:** Mi Seitelman/IDI **4/5:** Patrick Bunce **6:** Joe Cupido/IDI **7:** Ministry of Defence **89:** Patrick Bunce **10:** (top) MATRA: (bottom) US Air Force **11:** Erik Simonsen/IDI **12:** (top) Erick Simonsen/IDI: (bottom) Mi Seitelman/IDI **12/13:** US Air Force **13:** Brian Wolff/IDI **14:** (left) McDonnell Douglas: (right) Jonathan Scott **15:** Mi Seitelman/IDI **16:** (top) Jeremy Flack/API: (bottom) Ministry of Defence **17:** (top) British Aerospace: (bottom) US Air Force **18:** (top) Ministry of Defence: (bottom) British Aerospace **19:** (top) British Aerospace: (bottom) Ministry of Defence **20:** US Air Force **21:** (top) CASA: (centre) Aermacchi: (bottom) Austin J. Brown/APL **22:** (both) Dassault-Breguet **23:** British Aerospace **24:** via M. J. Hooks **25:** (top) Dassault-Breguet: (bottom) British Aerospace **26/27:** Austin J. Brown/APL **28:** US Air Force **29:** (top) Mi Seitelman/IDI: (bottom) US Air Force **30:** (both) US Air Force **31:** (top and right) Patrick Bunce: (bottom) US Air Force **32:** (top) US Air Force: (bottom) Mi Seitelman/IDI **33:** US Air Force **34/35:** US Navy **36:** (top) Patrick Bunce: (bottom) US Air Force **37:** (top) Mi Seitelman/IDI: (bottom) US Air Force **38:** (top) Chuck Mussi/IDI: (bottom) Canadian Forces **39:** Patrick Bunce **40:** (top) McDonnell Douglas: (bottom left and right) Patrick Bunce **41:** (top) Patrick Bunce: (bottom) Mi Seitelman/IDI **42/43:** (top) US Air Force: (bottom) McDonnell Douglas **43:** US Air Force **44/45:** (all) US Air Force **46/47** US Air Force **47:** (top) Boeing: (bottom) US Air Force **48/49:** (all) Fred Sutter/IDI **50/51:** (top) Kirby Harrison/IDI: (bottom) Fred Sutter/IDI **51:** US Air Force **52/53:** (top) US Air Force: (bottom) David Hathcox/IDI **54:** (both) Fred Sutter/IDI **55:** McDonnell Douglas **56:** Patrick Bunce **56/57:** Westland Helicopters **57:** Lindsay Peacock **58/59:** via IDI **60:** Jeremy

Flack/API **61:** (both) Frank Mormillo/IDI **62:** US Air Force **63:** (both) Jeremy Flack/API **64:** (top) Tim Laming: (bottom) Lindsay Peacock **65:** Smiths Industries **66/67:** Tim Laming **68:** Fred Sutter/IDI **69:** Jeremy Flack/API **70:** (top) Bell Helicopters: (bottom) Mi Seitelman/IDI **71:** Bell Helicopters **72/73:** (both) McDonnell Douglas **74:** (top) Brian Wolff/IDI: (bottom) McDonnell Douglas **74/75:** McDonnell Douglas **76:** Lindsay Peacock **77:** (both) Patrick Bunce **78:** Patrick Bunce **78/79:** Tim Laming **79:** Patrick Bunce **80:** British Aerospace **81:** (top) Panavia: (bottom) British Aerospace **82/83:** (all) Messerschmitt-Bolkow-Blohm **84/85:** Patrick Bunce **86:** (top) McDonnell Douglas: (bottom) US Air Force **87:** Mi Seitelman/IDI **88:** McDonnell Douglas **89:** (both) US Air Force **90:** Patrick Bunce **91:** (top) Patrick Bunce: (centre) Sqn. Ldr. J.D.Armstrong: (bottom) Gary Kieffer/IDI **92/93:** Austin J. Brown/APL **94:** Patrick Bunce **94/95:** Erick Simonsen/IDI **95:** Tim Laming **96:** US Air Force **97:** (top) Mi Seitelman/IDI: (bottom) Panavia **98:** US Air Force **99:** (top) McDonnell Douglas: (bottom) Jonathan Scott/IDI **100:** J. Dibbs

100/101: Patrick Bunce **101:** Patrick Bunce **102:** George Hall/IDI **103:** (top) George Hall/IDI: (centre) Grumman: (bottom) Frank Mormillo **104:** (top) Westland Helicopters: (bottom) Messerschmitt-Bolkow-Blohm **105:** (top) Aerospatiale: (bottom) Messerschmitt-Bolkow-Blohm **106:** Ministry of Defence **107:** (top) Mi Seitelman/IDI: (bottom) Ministry of Defence **108:** (top) British Aerospace: (bottom) Austin J. Brown/APL **109:** Patrick Bunce **110:** Austin J. Brown/APL **111:** (top) Mark Wagner/APL: (bottom) Austin J. Brown/APL **112:** George Hall/IDI **113:** (both) McDonnell Douglas **114:** (top) US Air Force: (bottom) Frank Mormillo/IDI **115:**

(top) Joe Cupido/IDI: (bottom) US Air Force **116:** (all) Jeremy Flack/API **117:** (both) Fred Sutter/IDI **118/119:** Lindsay Peacock **120:** US Air Force **120/121:** US Air Force **121:** Lindsay Peacock **122:** (top) McDonnell Douglas: (bottom) Jeremy Flack/API **123:** Cessna **124/125:** (top) Patrick Bunce: (bottom) US Air Force **125:** US Air Force **126/127:** (all) US Air Force **128:** (top) British Aerospace: (bottom) US Air Force **129:** (top) SAAB: (bottom) US Air Force **130:** (both) US Air Force **131:** (top) US Air Force: (bottom) McDonnell Douglas **132:** George Hall/IDI **133:** (top) McDonnell Douglas: (bottom) Mi Seitelman/IDI **134/135:** (all) Jeremy Flack/API **136:** McDonnell Douglas **137:** (top) McDonnell Douglas: (bottom) Mi Seitelman/IDI **138/139:** Frank Mormillo/IDI **140:** SAAB **141:** (top) Robert F. Dorr via Austin J. Brown/APL: (bottom) Austin J. Brown/APL **142:** (both) Aerospatiale **143:** (all) General Dynamics **144:** (top) US Air Force: (bottom) Messerschmitt-Bolkow-Blohm **145:** (top) US Air Force: (bottom) MATRA **146:** (top) Canadian Forces: (bottom) Agostino Von Hassell/IDI **147:** Hunting Engineering **148:** (top) Peter R. Foster: (bottom) British Aerospace **149:** Lindsay Peacock **150:** (top) US Navy: (bottom) US Air Force **151:** (top) Patrick Bunce: (bottom) US Air Force **152:** Jeremy Flack/API **153:** (top) David Hathcox/IDI: (bottom) Patrick Bunce **154/155:** (all) General Dynamics **156/157:** (both) Patrick Bunce **158/159:** US Air Force via IDI **160:** (both) McDonnell Douglas **161:** Mi Seitelman/IDI **162:** (both) US Air Force **162/163:** Dassault-Breguet.

Endpapers: F-111 formation
Page 1: Jaguar head-up display
2/3 A-10A Thunderbolt II firing gun
4/5: Tornado GR.1 take-off
6: A-7D Corsair approaching tanker
7: Harrier GR.3 formation
8/9: A-10A Thunderbolt II rear view
10: (top) Jaguar releasing laser-guided bombs: (bottom) OA-37Bs in formation
11: F-4 Phantom missile launch.

Introduction

AMONG THE many definitions of the word "strike" that may be found in contemporary dictionaries is one which says "attack, especially by aircraft". A simple summation that may be, but it would be hard to define the mission more precisely or more succinctly.

There are those, of course, who would remark that the definition given above is inadequate, arguing that it could be expanded to take account of the types of aircraft that may be called upon to fulfil the strike mission or, alternatively, the types of target. For the purposes of this volume, though, no attempt has been made to draw such fine distinction or limits.

Instead, it features examples of most of the many and varied types of aircraft that possess the ability to carry and deliver ordnance against surface targets. In addition, it also looks at some of the weapons that can now be employed, contemporary armament being almost as diverse as the aircraft that routinely perform strike missions.

With regard to defining strike aircraft, matters were simpler a few years ago, when it was possible to design and afford machines able to satisfy just one aspect of the panoply of aerial warfare. Today, when multi-mission capability is virtually

a pre-requisite, the distinctions have become blurred and one would indeed be hard pressed to identify a thoroughbred strike aircraft, at least as far as the armed forces of the West are concerned.

Certainly, a casual glance through the pages of this volume soon reveals that the strike mission may be undertaken by a hugely disparate (some might say motley) assortment of aircraft, with perhaps the only true practitioners being the "big bombers" — but who, apart from the USA and the USSR, can afford to buy those these days?

In consequence, the classification of strike aircraft has become almost baffling-ly broad, encompassing types which in the past would more properly have been described as trainers (British Aerospace Hawk and Cessna A-37 Dragonfly), fighters (McDonnell Douglas F-15 Eagle and Dassault Mirage 2000), helicopters (Westland Lynx and Bell AH-1 Huey-Cobra) and bombers (Boeing B-52 Stratofortress and Rockwell B-1B). A few moments spent in idle consideration will quickly confirm that these are indeed hugely different types, but it does rather beg the question as to whether they can all properly and accurately be described as strike aircraft.

If one accepts the premise that each and every one of the types depicted here is capable of attack — a premise that can hardly be denied — one has little option but to admit that they are. Certainly, each is able to deliver ordnance with great accuracy and potentially devastating results for anyone unlucky enough to be in the firing line at the moment of impact. As has ever been the case, bombs, rockets and missiles have no conscience (not even the latest generation of "smart" weapons), being concerned neither with the vehicle from which they are delivered nor, for that matter, with the target at which they are aimed.

If the weapons themselves are "dim", it

follows that so too, for much of the time, are the machines from which they are launched, dropped or fired. For the most part, it is these machines which form the stars of this volume but people perhaps tend to forget that, left to their own devices, they are benign and must remain firmly rooted to the ground. It is only when Man — the Strike Ace — occupies the cockpit and heads skywards that the capability for destruction can be fully realised and, sometimes, employed to its maximum devastating potential.

What of the strike aces themselves? What kind of people are they? Hollywood's perception is perhaps the one that is most familiar to "Joe Public". In the eyes of the movie world, the strike ace (and, indeed, his fighter pilot counterpart) is usually depicted as a ruggedly hand-

some and fast talking individual who divides his time between dealing out death and destruction and satisfying his monumental libido. A sort of snappy "Rambo"-type figure, if you like, but one that is perhaps just a touch more erudite and much less sweaty.

As is so often the case, Hollywood's vision misses the target completely, a failing that can never be levelled at the hero, whose bombs must be among the "smartest" around since they seem to possess the ability to ignore gravity and defy the laws of ballistics.

The reality is, of course, very different but it cannot be denied that the strike ace is in many ways a very special individual since the nature of his work is inherently hazardous for terra firma and gravity are both unforgiving of error. Entrusting his

continued well-being to a mass of electronic goodies as, perhaps under the cover of darkness, he performs a mock attack on an unseen target with nothing more offensive than a practice bomb, the strike ace faces risks that most of us are ignorant of and that virtually all of us would choose to avoid.

If tackled about the subject, the strike aces would probably play down the risk factor, preferring to emphasise their own skills as pilots and/or navigators. That reaction may be prompted by ego (like fighter pilots, strike pilots have egos too) but is probably best explained by the fact that "it goes with the territory". Put simply, the "it can't happen to me" philosophy must hold sway, as, indeed, it did in World War II.

There are some who would point to such an attitude as being indicative of arrogance, a conclusion that is perhaps not unreasonable and one that in certain cases is probably correct. It does, however, fail to take into account the fact that strike and fighter pilots invariably have a tremendous amount of faith in their own ability and that, too, is not unreasonable, since they can accurately be described as belonging to an elite body, membership of which is granted only to a select few. Certainly, the powers-that-be are most definitely not in the business of entrusting hugely expensive warplanes to idiots.

On the question of risk, then, I suspect that the truth is quite prosaic, perhaps encapsulated in the philosophy that, if one spends time contemplating risk, one is unlikely ever to attempt anything that is worthwhile. This is not to say that they ignore the hazards: that would indeed be foolhardy. But rather that they minimise them, something that can be achieved in several ways.

Training is without doubt the most important and it is perhaps not widely realised by the public that military pilots are in fact continually engaged in this activity, every sortie contributing further to building up the storehouse of knowledge that might, ultimately, one day make all the difference between life and death.

In large part, public perception seems to incline to the belief that once a pilot is qualified he is ready for almost anything. The reality is actually far removed, for achieving combat-ready status is merely a significant milestone in a pilot's career. It does not terminate his concern with train-

ing, for it is then necessary to stay "up to speed" in all of the disciplines which he has learnt. Weapons delivery techniques, gunnery, air-to-air refuelling, air combat and low level flight are just some of the skills involved in this process and are all constantly honed.

Zeroing in on just one of these disciplines, high-speed flight at low level is never an undertaking to be entered into lightly. If you happen to be watching from the ground when a flight of strike aircraft passes by at 500 feet (150m), you might well be excused for thinking that they are flying low. In fact, that sort of flight level is a relatively safe altitude and one at which even newly qualified pilots feel comfortable. In war, however, it would most definitely be unsafe for it greatly increases the amount of "exposure" time to poten-

tial enemy threats, modern defences being likely to exact an awful toll on anyone who comes within reach.

Thus, if one is to stand a reasonable chance of surviving long enough to be able to reach and attack one's target, it will be necessary to go lower so as to take maximum advantage of the cover offered by "terrain-masking" and, hopefully, deny enemy gun and missile crews the opportunity to "lock-on". The kind of level that we are now talking about is, in large part, a compromise aimed at minimising the risk of striking the ground while also limiting exposure to radar-directed guns and missiles.

With the RAF, the 100-foot (30m) mark seems to be most favoured, in so far as it permits crews to divide their attention between the twin threats of ground im-

pact and enemy action. There is, however, a world of difference between these two levels, which is perhaps best exemplified by the fact that, at 100 feet, even a commonplace hiccough or sneeze could have lethal consequences for pilot and navigator alike.

Those whose piloting skills are mainly concerned with aerial combat tend to view their air-to-ground orientated counterparts with considerable disdain, often contemptuously dismissing them as "mud-movers". It's a colourful term . . . it may even be an accurate one . . . but it fails to do justice to the Strike Aces. It is to be hoped that this volume will perhaps go some way towards redressing that fact while simultaneously advising "Joe Public" that such skills are hard won and even harder to maintain.

Given appropriate lighting effects — whether they be natural or studio originated — fixed and rotary-wing aircraft can provide powerful and, at times, almost surreal subject matter for the imaginative photographer. Clockwise, from right, the subjects of these distinctive shots are the AH-64A Apache, the F-4 Phantom, the F-15 Eagle and the AV-8B Harrier II.

Delivery of ordnance is the *raison d'etre* of strike aircraft and calls for precise flying skills on the part of the pilot. Methods of delivery may vary considerably but all take into account the ballistic properties of the weapon being used. From left to right, the prototype F-15E Strike Eagle, an F-111A and two F/A-18A Hornets deposit bombs on targets far below during the course of test and training missions in the USA.

In the modern era, when defences are formidable, low-level flight is one of the primary tactics used in evading detection and the risk of destruction both before and after an attack. Here, four very different types demonstrate low-level capability. Clockwise from the right, they are a Pucara which was evaluated in Britain after the Falklands conflict, an RAF Harrier GR.1 in arctic paint scheme for an exercise in Norway, a B-52G Stratofortress of SAC's 97th Bomb Wing, and a brace of Luftwaffe Tornados.

British Aerospace's Hawk is probably the most potent of the current generation of light strike aircraft. In RAF service, it functions as an advanced trainer, a job which includes initial weapons delivery instruction (above left, above and right). The single-seat Hawk 200 (below left) is even more capable, being a dedicated attack model with extra stores stations and more sophisticated avionics.

Types employed on the strike mission have proliferated in the past couple of decades, when many jet trainers have been adapted to perform light attack duties with a number of air arms around the world. Well suited for nations with limited financial resources or for use in low-threat areas, such types include Cessna's A-37B Dragonfly (left), CASA's Aviojet (right, top) and the Aermacchi Veltro II (right, centre). In the same class dimensionally but much heavier, AMX (right, bottom) is the outcome of a joint venture between Brazil and Italy and is purpose-built for the attack role although it too is classed as a light strike aircraft.

Further evidence of the potent nature of the modern trainer is provided by the Franco-German Alpha Jet. An aircraft in pure trainer configuration (left) contrasts with the Lancier strike version (above), the latter being compatible with a variety of air-to-air and air-to-surface weapons as well as also possessing a gun pod beneath its belly. Of a much earlier generation, the British Aerospace Strikemaster (right) is markedly inferior when it comes to armament capability, this Royal New Zealand Air Force example carrying just two rocket pods but it may also employ bombs or gun packs on the underwing stations.

Contrasting approaches to the light strike theme are apparent in these studies of three such types — the CASA C.101 Aviojet (left) and British Aerospace Hawk 200 (below right), both opt for a low-mounted wing, while the Dassault Breguet/Dornier Alpha Jet (above right) features a shoulder-mounted arrangement. All three began life as pure trainers and all have subsequently been subjected to further development so as to boost strike potential. Capability of each of these three types is broadly similar, weapons options including bombs, air-to-air and air-to-surface missiles and guns, although the Hawk 200 probably has the edge in terms of performance and certainly offers a more complex array of avionics.

(Overleaf) Used as an advanced trainer by the RAF, the Hawk is perhaps better known as the mount of the Red Arrows, one of their aircraft being caught against a lurid sky as it goes through its display routine.

There are few aircraft anywhere that are as deficient in appeal as the Fairchild-Republic A-10A Thunderbolt II but its lack of grace doesn't detract from the fact that it is a machine to be reckoned with. Almost everything about it is big and bulky and even the relatively simple act of replenishing the GAU-8/A Avenger 30mm cannon magazine calls for use of muscle to move the outsize loading equipment into place.

Although perhaps best known as a tank-killer par excellence, the A-10A Thunderbolt II is no mean machine when it comes to close air support, being able to carry a healthy payload of conventional ordnance. Bombs, like the parachute retarded devices shown being delivered in this sequence, naturally figure highly in its arsenal but it may also utilise sub-munitions dispensers, napalm and guided missiles, as well as the fearsome GAU-8/A Avenger 30mm cannon.

Not for nothing is the Fairchild Republic A-10 Thunderbolt II more commonly known as the "Wart Hog", for it must surely rank as being one of the most distinctive (some would say ugly) combat aircraft of the present day. It must also be one of the most formidable, by virtue of the integral GAU-8/A Avenger 30mm cannon, the muzzle of which is seen on a fearsomely-marked A-10A of the Air Force Reserve (below left) and in company with a pilot in full flight kit (right). Able to spew out milk bottle-sized shells at a terrifying rate, gases virtually envelop the A-10A when the gun is fired (left).

Good visibility is a subject of vital concern to any military pilot. Regardless of whether he is a "strike ace" or merely the "driver" of an interceptor, he needs to be able to see clearly and it would not be overstating the case to say that it could make the difference between life and death in a hostile situation. Ground crew are well aware of the need to be able to see clearly and, as seen here, devote much time to the polishing of canopies and removing blemishes.

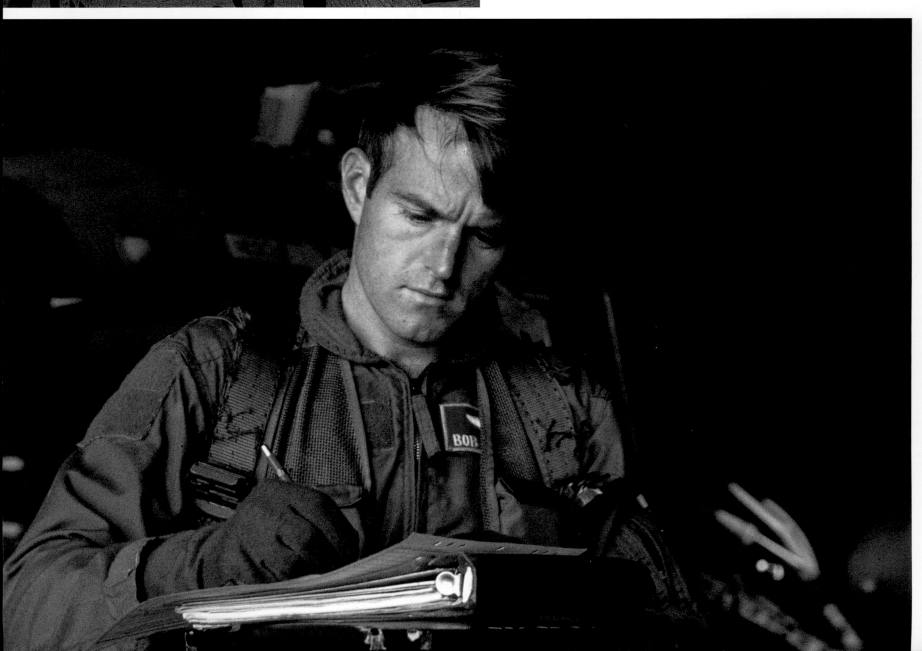

Preparations for flight are a lengthy business, beginning with the planning process which may take two hours or more. It is also necessary to don special clothing designed to help crews withstand the rigours of high-speed flight and to survive in the event of ejection, epitomised here by a Tornado crew (opposite page, upper). Paperwork also has to be attended to before flight, a USAF pilot dealing with this matter (opposite page, lower). Encumbered by personal kit, even boarding is potentially hazardous, as shown by an F-4 navigator (left). Once in the cockpit there are still more jobs to be done before heading for the runway; here an RAF Harrier pilot pauses to study his maps before leaving the hide (above).

One of the last actions before entering the cockpit is a pre-flight inspection to ensure the aircraft is safe to fly. In this sequence, a US Navy KA-6D Intruder crew prepare to man the cockpit (left, top), a Canadian pilot inspects a two-seat CF-18B (left, bottom) and an EF-111A crewman studies the exhaust nozzle of one of the Raven's two Pratt & Whitney TF30 turbofan engines (above).

nature, but great care must still be taken to ensure that the drills are correctly observed.

Although still very much employed in the nuclear deterrent role, the veteran Stratofortress has gained new conventional warfare missions in recent times. One such task is maritime-related and suitably configured examples of the B-52G now fulfil anti-ship duties with weapons such as the Harpoon air-to-surface missile, shown carried beneath the wing of a B-52G (left). Mines may also be dispensed from the bomb bay (above left), with SAC units engaged in this duty flying from bases such as Loring, Maine and Andersen, Guam, where a B-52G is shown on final approach (above).

At more than a dozen Strategic Air Command bases throughout the continental USA and on Guam, B-52 nuclear-armed bombers still stand on alert, ready to launch at a moment's notice in the event of the Emergency War Order being promulgated. In this sequence of pictures depicting facets of the nuclear "business", we see a SAC bomber crew racing to a "Buff" during an alert exercise, the view from inside the cockpit during a low-level trip down one of the special "Olive Branch" routes and a Stratofortress on its way to the target area closing to receive fuel from a KC-135 Stratotanker somewhere over the USA.

As well as gravity nuclear bombs, the Stratofortress is able to employ nuclear-tipped missiles such as the Boeing products shown on the opposite page. The AGM-69 Short Range Attack Missile or SRAM (top) entered SAC's arsenal in summer 1972 and was followed a decade later by the AGM-86 Air Launched Cruise Missile or ALCM (bottom). It is the job of the ''Buff's'' crew to carry them to a point where they can be released, and accurate navigation is vital if the weapons are to have a chance of finding their targets. Responsibility for this falls to the Navigator and Radar Navigator who occupy the ''Hell Hole'' as the lower crew compartment is often called.

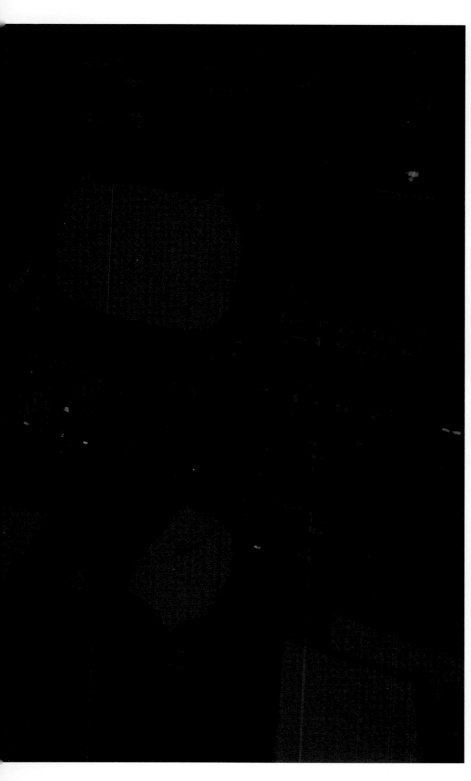

Now well into its third decade of operational service, the Boeing B-52 Stratofortress is still an important part of Strategic Air Command. Best known as a nuclear bomber, it may also fulfil conventional missions as portrayed to right and left by a B-52H depositing a gaggle of retarded bombs on a desert range. It, too, uses aerial refuelling to extend its range, a B-52H being seen closing to make contact with a tanker (above).

EXPLOSIVES A

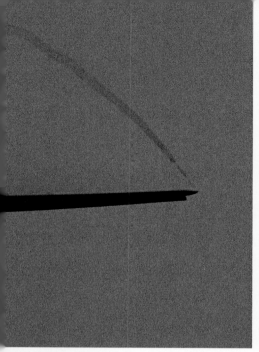

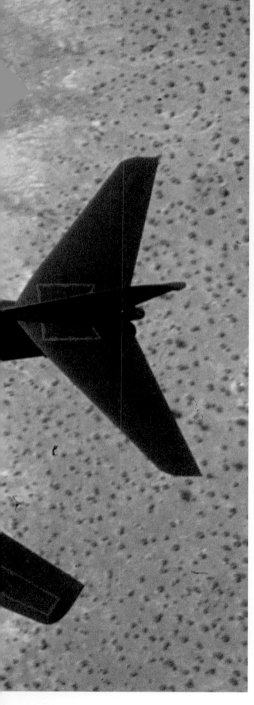

With the afterburners glowing amidst a haze of heat vapour generated by four General Electric F101 turbofan engines working at full power, a B-1B gets airborne (left, upper) at the start of a training sortie which will include simulated bomb delivery and a low level "Olive Branch" run. Built by Rockwell, the B-1B has yet to reach its full potential as an operational bomber with the Strategic Air Command. Despite the problems, its purposeful lines are seen to advantage in these views of a B-1B flying low above the desert (left) and closing to make contact with a tanker for additional fuel (above).

Possessing versatility perhaps only surpassed by the famed Dakota, the Lockheed Hercules proved itself a most fearsome weapon of war in Vietnam, where "gunship" conversions scored heavily in interdiction of the Ho Chi Minh Trail. Two "Spectre" variants are seen here, the original AC-130A (above) and the AC-130H (below). The latter is easily the most heavily armed model and includes a 105mm howitzer in its arsenal.

Although ground forces will still figure in the anti-armour battle, they will receive assistance from the sky. Anti-tank helicopters essentially fall into two classes with differences relating mainly to crew protection. The MBB PAH-1 (right and below) and the Hughes 500MD Defender (opposite) typify the lightly-protected "gunship", PAH-1 using six Euromissile HOT weapons while Defender has four Hughes BGM-71 TOWs. Acquisition and tracking is achieved with the aid of a special sight. On the PAH-1 this is fitted on the cabin roof while the Defender uses a nose-mounted sight, which in theory will make it more likely to be observed by an alert enemy.

(Overleaf) Dedicated battlefield helicopters may be expensive but they are a growing breed. One of the newest additions to the list is Italy's Agusta A129 Mangusta, seen here letting fly with a Hughes BGM-71 TOW missile during development testing. In the front cockpit, a gunner uses the sighting device which guides TOW to its target.

Ultra low-level "nap-of-earth" flying is almost a matter of routine for Britain's Army Air Corps, and the Lynx helicopter is in many ways an ideal vehicle, being reasonably fast and highly agile in the hands of a skilled and confident pilot (left and right). Although normally fitted with the Hughes BGM-71 TOW anti-tank missile, Lynx is actually compatible with a variety of weapons, such as the unguided air-to-surface SURA rockets seen being fired in a fairly steep diving attitude (below).

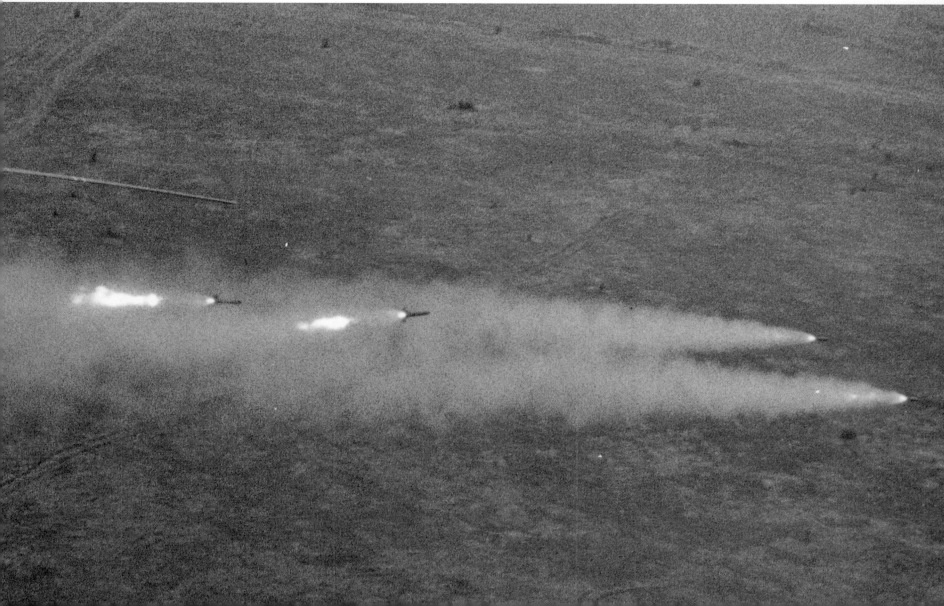

Since the desire to maximise weapons payload can often only be achieved at the penalty of fuel, in-flight refuelling has become increasingly important as a means of extending range. Although not favoured by the US Air Force which is probably the world's major exponent of transferring fuel in flight, the probe-and-drogue method is nevertheless widely used and is perhaps more versatile in that "buddy" packs may be "hung" on virtually all combat types. Jaguar (left), Skyhawk (above) and Intruder (right) are shown receiving fuel in this manner.

Both types of air refuelling technique are seen here, the USAF-preferred "flying boom" method being employed to allow a Phantom to take a "drink" from a Strategic Air Command KC-10A Extender (left) while three other F-4s await their turn. The alternative drogue concept is illustrated by Arctic-camouflaged Harriers (a GR.3 right and a T.4 below right) of the RAF receiving a "top-up" from a VC-10 tanker. Again, other elements of the formation fly nearby as they stand-by to take on fuel.

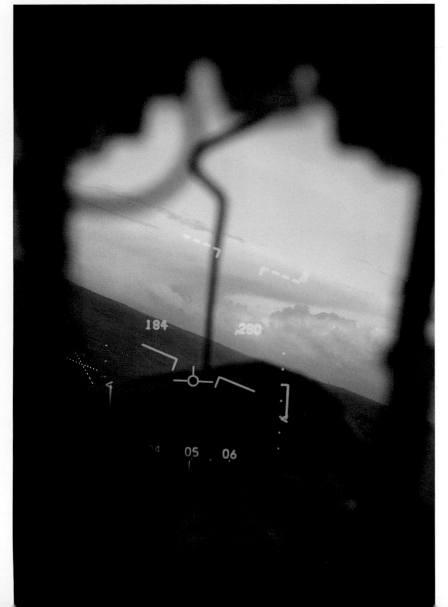

Modern technology means that virtually all combat types now feature a head-up display unit to aid the pilot, although the complexity of these may vary considerably. Framed by the canopy explosive cord, the Hawk (above) features nothing more than a gunsight reticle. In the Jaguar, a full HUD is provided, horizon and attitude indications being shown (left) during final approach to RAF Coltishall. Meanwhile, the Harrier pilot steering his way through a valley (right) also benefits from a comprehensive HUD.

The business of placing two aircraft in close proximity during flight is always a potentially risky one, hence the emphasis that is placed on formation flying during the earliest stages of the pilot training programme. Pictured against an angry-looking sky, an RAF Hawk heads for home at the end of a training sortie.

Purpose-built "gunships" are much tougher machines, epitomised by the Bell AH-1 HueyCobra which was the first true example of the breed. Originally lacking a really "heavy" punch, the Cobra has been much updated since it entered service in the mid-1960s and is indeed a most formidable helicopter, possessing true anti-armour capability in the shape of the BGM-71 TOW. Improvements have not been confined to armament for it now incorporates the obligatory head-up display unit as well as defensive "kit" such as radar warning receivers, chaff and infra-red flares.

Ever more bizarre items of kit are beginning to appear, with the devices mcdelled here by members of helicopter gunship crews being intended to permit them to operate more easily in a "head-up" rather than a "head-down" mode. This is one of several on-going initiatives which are intended to enhance tactical awareness in and around the battlefield.

In the world of the contemporary helicopter gunship, the Apache surely stands supreme, combining an impressive armament capability with quite remarkable agility. In head-on aspect, it can hardly be described as the most elegant of warplanes but aesthetic concerns are unlikely to be of interest to an opponent faced with eight Hellfire anti-armour missiles, 38 2.75in (7cm) rockets and a 30mm Chain Gun.

Without doubt the most potent expression of the helicopter gunship yet to see service in the West, the US Army's AH-64A Apache is compatible with an impressive array of weaponry. For "tank-busting", the anti-armour Hellfire missile is the principal weapon, launch of one of these being seen at left. The Apache can also tote a large number of unguided aerial rockets (above left and right) which can inflict considerable damage upon anyone unlucky enough to get in the way.

When not in their natural element, Tornados assigned to operational RAF squadrons spend most of their time hidden from view in individual shelters designed to provide protection from the risk of destruction by enemy bombs (opposite). Servicing, arming and fuelling activities are routinely performed in such shelters. Once outside the shelter, little time is wasted in getting airborne, illustrated by a pilot and navigator of the Luftwaffe preparing to take-off (left), and a clutch of No.9 Squadron machines heading for Bruggen's runway (below). Practice bomb carriers are carried beneath the belly of the last aircraft in the line.

Tip vortices stream from a Tactical Weapons Conversion Unit Tornado GR.1 as it is put through its paces for the benefit of the public at an air show (above), while the variable geometry wing of the Tornado is seen at maximum and minimum sweep settings on No.27 Squadron aircraft (below and left).

The result of a collaborative venture between Britain, Italy and West Germany, Tornado is indeed a most potent machine, capable of operating with an almost bewildering array of ordnance, including the JP233 sub-munitions dispenser seen here on an RAF development aircraft (above and right) and the broadly similar MW-1 which is used by the Luftwaffe.

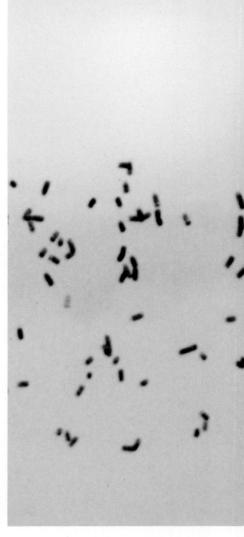

Considerable effort and money has been expended on development of the so-called "scatter" weapons in the past few years, devices of this type being optimised for use against a variety of targets such as airfields, armour and troop concentrations. West Germany's MW-1 area denial system intended for use by Tornado is typical, the bulky belly-mounted container housing either 4,536 KB44 anti-armour hollow-charge bomblets or 872 MIFF anti-tank mines. Lateral ejection of these sub-munitions results in a wide swathe of land being covered.

(Overleaf) Like the F-15, Dassault's Mirage 2000 has spawned a dedicated two-seat strike derivative, the 2000N model being optimised for long-range attack missions and relying on terrain-following radar for sustained flight at low-level. It also possesses the ability to carry and launch the stand-off ASMP nuclear weapon.

Perceived by many as the West's most outstanding air superiority fighter, the McDonnell Douglas Eagle is now adding strike to its impressive repertoire. The first production F-15E Strike Eagle is featured here with AIM-7 Sparrow AAMs (left, bottom) and AGM-65 Maverick air-to-surface missiles (above). Also visible are LANTIRN night nav/attack system pods. At Seymour-Johnson, North Carolina, the 4th Tactical Fighter Wing is the first fully operational unit to receive the F-15E (left, top).

Still the primary weapon intended for delivery by strike aircraft, the humble bomb is now available in a variety of forms to satisfy special requirements. "Slicks", such as those being deposited by the F-15 Strike Eagle prototype (left) are the least costly and probably least accurate. Greater precision can be achieved with "retards" of either the folding-fin or, as seen here (above and right), parachute types. Both of these devices delay impact and permit the attacking aircraft to move well clear before they detonate.

Much maligned during its early years of service as a result of mechanical malfunctions and less than ideal avionic sub-system performance figures, the F-111 eventually matured into a fine strike aircraft and is now generally viewed with approbation by those whose job it is to fly it. Examples of the "Aardvark", as it is colloquially and affectionately known, are shown here in landing configuration (left and right), in overseas service with the Royal Australian Air Force (centre right), and down low at the sort of altitude it would use if ever called upon to go to war (bottom right).

To be truly effective, today's strike aircraft should possess the ability to operate by both day and night in all kinds of weather conditions. One of the few types with this potential is the General Dynamics F-111, seen here against an ominous looking backdrop of cloud and sky.

In terms of sheer spectacle, the General Dynamics F-111 is usually perceived as being among the "second division" of air show performers but it does have one interesting trick in its limited repertoire. As demonstrated by an Australian "Aardvark", "torching" entails dumping fuel into the afterburner plume and is indeed a spectacular sight (above). Given the right conditions, such as a fairly tight turn in a relatively damp atmosphere, both the F-111 (left) and the Tornado (right) can provide visually striking images, since both types may generate quite noticeable wing tip vortices.

Rather differing capabilities are possessed by the aircraft shown here, the Cessna OA-37B Dragonfly (left) being a light attack type which is now used by the USAF as a forward air control platform, while the Mirage 2000 (above) and the Tornado GR.1 (below) are both considerably more potent, able to employ either conventional or thermonuclear weaponry.

The cockpit is almost invariably a cramped and confining place of work, freedom of movement being constrained by the multiplicity of harnesses and hoses that are necessary if crews are to perform efficiently.

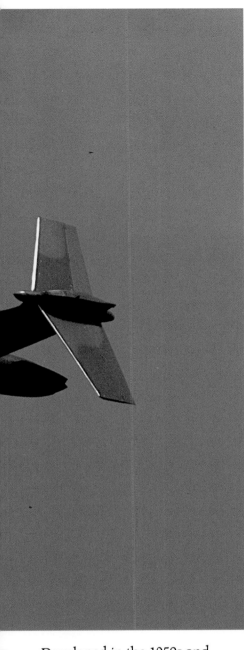

Developed in the 1950s and optimised for maritime attack with Britain's Fleet Air Arm, the Buccaneer successfully made the transition from being a sea-based type to a land-based one and it continues to serve with two Royal Air Force squadrons today, rather ironically being mainly employed in the maritime strike role. Elegant it may not be, but at low level there are few aircraft that can match it for sheer speed and even fewer that could hope to outrun it.

Despite the fact that the design dates back to the late 1950s, the Grumman Intruder is still a most potent strike aircraft and one that will form an important element of Navy and Marine Corps air power until the next century. Forward fuselage detail and the nose-mounted sensor turret are seen on a Navy A-6E (above) while Navy and Marine Intruders with a mixture of "slick" and "retard" bombs are shown on the opposite page.

Sea strike is no longer the sole prerogative of fixed-wing aircraft. Helicopters like the Sea Eagle-armed Westland Sea King (left) and the Exocet-capable Aerospatiale Super Puma (right) are able to administer crippling blows to any vessel unfortunate enough to come within range. Sea-skimming missiles like these and the USA's AGM-84 Harpoon possess tremendous penetrative power, demonstrated here by a Kormoran homing on to and impacting a redundant warship (below and below right).

Not since the advent of the first jet fighter has a particular type revolutionised aerial warfare in quite the same way as the V/STOL Harrier. Possessing the ability to operate away from major bases with only minimal support, it can quite literally disappear into the undergrowth as the pictures presented here illustrate. Taken during a field training exercise in West Germany, they show an engine change being accomplished in a temporary hangar (left), a pilot leaving his aircraft at the completion of a sortie (right) and ground troops doing routine pre-flight checks on a two-seater of No.3 Squadron (below). Such scenes are typical of any "off-base" deployment undertaken by elements of the Harrier force.

Comparison of these pictures will soon reveal notable differences between examples of the first and second generations of the Harrier "family". The RAF's new GR.5 has more stores stations, relocated outriggers and a revised cockpit layout but there is no disguising the similarity between it and the older GR.3 (left and above). In terms of capability, however, the GR.5 is infinitely superior at close air support and battlefield air interdiction.

Despite its unique abilities, the Harrier was still viewed as being little more than a costly "toy" by many senior officers in the military hierarchy until quite recently. The Sea Harrier changed that in the 1982 battle for the Falklands when it revealed great prowess in air combat and also made a number of bombing attacks on Argentinian positions. The Sea Harriers shown here were all photographed in the post-conflict era and include one about to take-off using the "ski-jump" at Yeovilton (above).

Progressive development of the British Harrier V/STOL warplane has led to the advent of the much more capable AV-8B which was evolved largely in response to the US Marine Corps' desire for superior payload potential and genuine VTOL characteristics. Also in service with the Royal Air Force as the Harrier GR.5, it is now the USMC's principal light attack aircraft and is indeed admirably suited for that service's traditional mission of close air support of ground forces.

Camouflage has always been a key concern of aircraft employed in the strike role but the past decade has been one of near constant change as air arms try to make their warplanes less visible. Nowhere has this process been more evident than in the USA and some of the variations tried are seen here. Moving clockwise from the right, these portray an Air National Guard F-16A and A-7D from an Arizona-based training unit, B-52s of the Strategic Air Command, Marine A-6E Intruders from all-weather attack squadron VMA(AW)-121 and F-4E Phantoms of the 3rd Tactical Fighter Wing at Clark Air Base in the Philippines.

Individualistic nose art is something that tends to appear sporadically, despite the best efforts of the authorities to stamp it out; but there is little doubt that it can have a positive effect on morale while simultaneously causing great offence to feminists. The three examples on this page appeared on F-111Es (top and bottom) and an FB-111A (centre) while those opposite adorned B-52Gs of the 2nd Bomb Wing at Barksdale AFB, Louisiana.

(Overleaf) Viewed in silhouette against a rather lurid early morning sky, a B-52G Stratofortress tucks away its undercarriage at the start of a training sortie. Such missions regularly last up to ten hours and usually include at least one aerial refuelling as well as a low-level sector and a simulated attack. Radar bomb scoring is used to assess accuracy.

Although it no longer occupies a position of dominance in the size league, the B-52 Stratofortress is still a fairly hefty piece of machinery and one that requires considerable skill on the part of the pilot during the approach and landing regime. Moving clockwise from the right, we see a "Buff" with its gear down and flaps and spoilers deployed as it nears the runway; a B-52 beginning to decelerate with the aid of the massive braking parachute seconds after making a "four-pointer" landing and, finally, a head-on view of a Stratofortress during a cross-wind landing with the undercarriage slewed at an angle so as to keep the aircraft "flying into wind".

While they make for attractive pictures, line-ups like these are seldom seen at operational front-line air bases these days. On the opposite page, a trio of two-seater Hornets from VFA-125 head a line which also includes a single-seat F/A-18A from Navy operational test and evaluation squadron VX-4 (above), while crew access ladders rest against the nose sections of Harrier T.4 two-seaters serving with No.233 Operational Conversion Unit at RAF Wittering (below). Lastly, three A-37B Dragonflies laden with underwing fuel tanks wait to be delivered from Cessna's production facility to a Latin American customer (left).

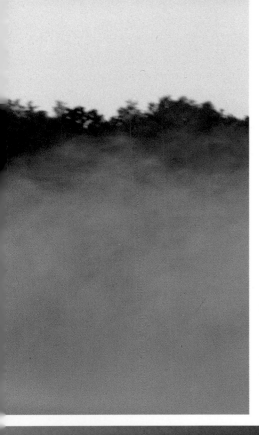

Take-off is an awfully noisy but impressive spectacle since virtually all modern strike aircraft rely on afterburner to get airborne. Two famous US types are seen employing this power-boosting aid, an F-4 roaring off into a Korean sunset (below right) and an F-16 displaying its sprightly field performance at Farnborough (left), while (below) two "Wild Weasel" F-4Gs await clearance to begin their take-off roll at George AFB, California.

Many modern bombs can be fitted with precision guidance systems to permit them to be employed with great accuracy. One such device is the GBU-15 which consists of a cruciform wing and tail package that is added to the base weapon which may be either the Mk.84 2,000lb bomb or the SUU-54 sub-munitions dispenser. Electro-optical (TV) or imaging infra-red guidance may be used to provide day or night capability. Here, an F-4E Phantom of the 3rd TFW releases a bomb-based GBU-15 (above), the weapon's accuracy being graphically portrayed by a GBU-15 homing on and striking a target (left and right).

Air-delivered weaponry comes in many different types, each ideal for use on a specific objective. Napalm, seen being dropped by two Marine Harriers (above) is still particularly effective against "soft" targets such as troops. For "hard" targets, such as the emplacement (left), laser and TV-guided bombs are highly effective and (right) remarkably accurate, while anti-armour weapons include Sweden's RBS56 missile which is shown scoring a direct hit on a redundant tank (right, above).

Good formation flying is a skill which must be mastered by all strike pilots, even though they may only rarely be called upon to employ such expertise. Formations like these are unlikely ever to be employed in the event of combat but they do provide impressive opportunities for the airborne photographer to show his skill. Clockwise from above, they depict Air National Guard A-10A "Wart Hogs"; a mixed F-16, F-111, F-15 and A-10 group from the 57th Fighter Weapons Wing; a quartet of F/A-18A Hornets from Navy training squadron VFA-125; and an F-16C and F-4G SAM-suppression team from the 52nd TFW.

No other service has greeted the Hornet's multi-mission potential quite as warmly as the US Marine Corps, whose operating doctrine places great emphasis on the dual fighter-attack role. Perhaps the only failing is the lack of VTOL capability but the Marines are at least able to call upon the AV-8B Harrier II. A mix of missiles and bombs are carried by the Hornets depicted here, weapons on display including the AGM-88A HARM anti-radiation missile (right, top).

Despite the arguments which surround its much-vaunted dual mission capability, the Hornet is without doubt an impressive air show performer and one that invariably causes heads to turn in its direction as it runs through its routine. The subject of this collection is a Canadian CF-18A which appeared at Farnborough and another "hot ship" of an earlier era — the de Havilland D.H.88 Comet — is visible in the departure view.

US Navy and Marine Corps air power has been greatly boosted by the F/A-18 Hornet which is almost equally adept at strike and pure fighter tasks, hence the decision to redesignate Navy light attack units (VA) as fighter-attack outfits (VFA) on conversion to the Hornet. Below, three aircraft from the west coast training unit VFA-125 fly low over the desert while a fourth bomb-laden example watches from above during a simulated "Alpha" strike. Bombs of the retarded type are carried by the VFA-86 machines which also feature AIM-9L Sidewinder missiles (right), while two Marine aircraft from VMFA-531 deposit bombs on a desert target (below right).

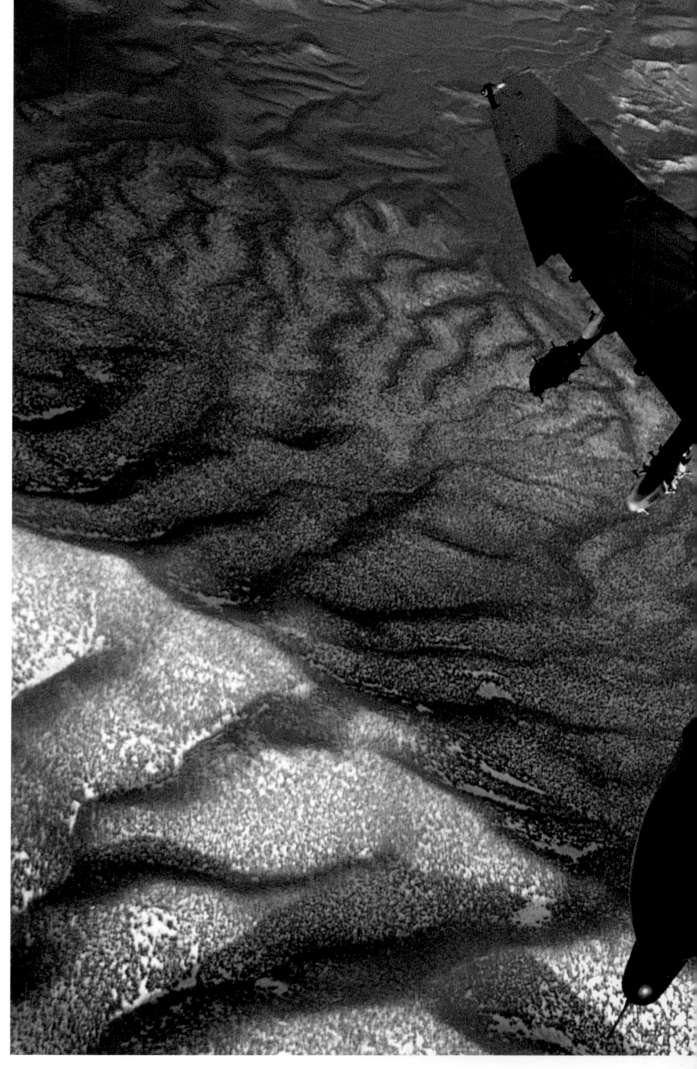

Of all strike-related tasks, the job of defence suppression is arguably the most hazardous since it requires exponents to be "first in, last out" over the battle area. Following on from the F-100 and F-105, the "Iron Hand" suppression task of the USAF is now undertaken by the F-4G Phantom. A much modified machine, it has a complex array of sensors to detect and identify enemy SAM sites and may use a variety of weapons, such as Shrike and HARM missiles or cluster bomb units, to knock them out.

Maintaining strict neutrality has not prevented Sweden's relatively small aerospace industry from evolving a succession of superb warplanes. Tailored to fulfil the unique requirements of Sweden's Flygvapnet, the Viggen is indeed an outstanding machine, combining splendid short-field performance with true multimission potential and able to operate as a strike aircraft against targets on both land and sea. Distinctive it may be, but its unusual shape is no bar to performing reconnaissance or interceptor functions.

Air-to-surface missiles such as those depicted here form a costly but valuable element of the arsenal which may be used by the contemporary strike aircraft to engage "hard" targets. Despite entering service as long ago as 1960, Aerospatiale's AS.30 is still in production in a much improved laser-guided version, seen on launch from a Mirage F.1 (above) and impacting on a target (left). On the opposite page, the sequence of pictures portrays a Hughes AGM-65 Maverick launch by a General Dynamics F-16B Fighting Falcon. Variants of this weapon use imaging infra-red, TV and laser guidance systems.

As well as weapons intended for use against the more conventional types of ground target, the air-to-surface missile classification also includes anti-radar devices. Intended to counter the threat posed by surface-to-air missile sites, they home on radiation put out by ground tracking radars for missile guidance. Weapons in this category include ALARM (left), ARMAT (right) and the AGM-88 HARM (above left and above).

In addition to good old-fashioned "iron bombs" and "smart" weapons, strike aircraft are equally versatile at delivering other no less nasty devices. Rockets such as those being launched from a Canadian CF-18B (above left) still figure highly in the global arsenal, as does the cluster bomb unit deposited by an A-4 Skyhawk (left). Even more effective if delivered accurately is the JP233 which contains area denial mines and (above) cratering devices.

Serving with three front-line RAF
units, the Jaguar GR.1 fulfils strike
and tactical reconnaissance tasks.
No. 41 Squadron is the only recce
outfit and is represented here by
an Arctic camouflaged example
(above left), painted for
deployment to Norway, and a
machine in standard colours
(above). Strike Jaguars are
epitomised by a former RAF
Germany aircraft laden with laser-
guided 1,000lb bombs.

Specialised ground equipment may often be used to ease the task of the munitions specialists who are responsible for loading items of ordnance. Here, a variety of weapon carrying devices are employed to install bombs on an A-10 (left), a GBU-15 cruciform glide bomb on an F-4E (right, lower) and a Maverick air-to-surface missile on an A-10 (right, upper). Nevertheless, good old fashioned muscle-power is still sometimes the only way, particularly on aircraft carriers (above) where space is limited.

Among the unsung heroes of the strike world are the munitions specialists whose job it is to manhandle the invariably bulky and often exceedingly heavy items of ordnance into place. Arduous in the extreme, it often entails muscle-wrenching effort and is also a potentially hazardous task, for a moment's carelessness could have devastating consequences for personnel and aircraft alike.

Improvement programmes steadily add to the F-16's potential. The new Night Falcon version, shown with Maverick missiles (right), incorporates Lantirn night/all-weather attack equipment while the four 57th Fighter Weapons Wing F-16Cs (above) carry an assortment of ordnance. The original F-16A also remains in use and is seen depositing a quartet of "slick" bombs (above right).

Like the contemporary Hornet, the General Dynamics F-16 Fighting Falcon is a star performer on the air show circuit. Smoke generator equipment located in dummy AIM-9 Sidewinder air-to-air missiles as well as liberal use of the F-100 turbofan's afterburner result in a highly visible and impressively noisy routine when the aircraft is flown aggressively by skilled pilots. These two studies show an F-16C display at Farnborough.

(Overleaf) The Fighting Falcon's ability as an air show performer perhaps tends to draw attention away from the fact that it is essentially employed on air-to-ground tasks by the US Air Forces in Europe. In training, no such apparent contradiction is allowed. Pilots like this member of the 50th Tactical Fighter Wing at Hahn spend much of their time in perfecting the art of depositing bombs on target.